I SPY HALLOWEEN

A FUN HOLIDAY GUESSING ACTIVITY BOOK, INTERACTIVE I SPY HALLOWEEN ADVENTURE FOR TODDLERS, PRESCHOOL AND KINDERGARTEN

To Everyone Enjoying the Halloween Spirit This Year!

Hey Parents! Ready to make this Halloween extra special? We've got a spooktacular treat just for you and your little one!

10 FREE Coloring Pages!

Your child will love these exclusive coloring pages filled with friendly monste playful witches, and magical Halloween scenes—all inspired by our book. It's the perfect way to keep the Halloween spirit alive and boost creativity!

Getting them is easy:

Just scan the QR code below to instantly download your free pages. It's fast, simple, and sure to bring smiles all around!

Don't wait—unlock more Halloween fun now!
Discover More Halloween Magic Here!

HOW TO PLAY ?

TRY TO GUESS THE HIDDEN PICTURE AT EACH CHALLENGE AND COLOR IT, THEN TURN THE PAGE TO REVEAL THE ANSWER. MAY YOUR HALLOWEEN ADVENTURE BE FILLED WITH EXCITEMENT, DISCOVERY AND LEARNING NEW VOCABULY! GOOD LUCK!

Want More Fun & Free Resources?

Unlock 10 exclusive bonus coloring pages, fun activities
all inspired by I Spy Halloween & early access to new books!
It's the perfect way to boost and spark your child creativity!
Simply scan this QR cide or visit:

kerriwenna.com

Your feedback means a lot!

Share your thoughts and help other parents find it!
Scan the QR code below to Leave us a quick review
and let us know What is your impression of the book.

Leaving a quick review helps other parents find this book.
Here's how to do it in 30 seconds:

1. Open your camera app.
2. Point it at the QR code on the right.
3. Boom! The review page opens instantly!

Thanks for being awesome and supporting a small indie
publisher like me! Your feedback makes a huge difference
and helps me create more fun books your kids will love.

THIS BOOK
BELONGS TO:

_____

- - - - - - - - - - - - - - - -

_____

I SPY WITH MY LITTLE EYE
SOMETHING STARTING WITH THE LETTER

It's an Acorn

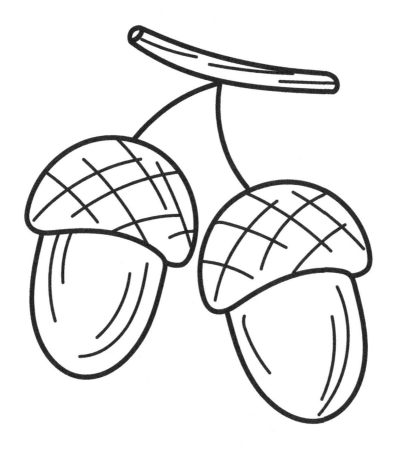

I SPY WITH MY LITTLE EYE SOMETHING STARTING WITH THE LETTER

It's a Broomstick

I SPY WITH MY LITTLE EYE
SOMETHING STARTING WITH THE LETTER

It's a
Cauldron

I SPY WITH MY LITTLE EYE
SOMETHING STARTING WITH THE LETTER

It's a Dinosaur

I SPY WITH MY LITTLE EYE
SOMETHING STARTING WITH THE LETTER

It's
Eyeballs

I SPY WITH MY LITTLE EYE
SOMETHING STARTING WITH THE LETTER

It's a Fangs

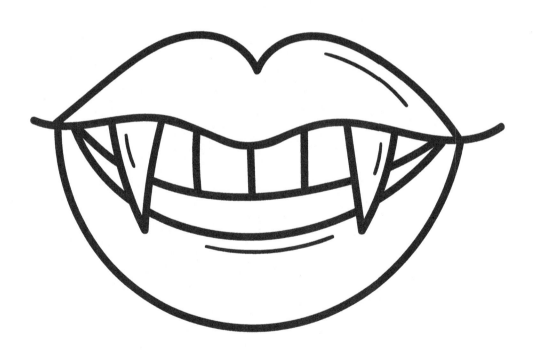

I SPY WITH MY LITTLE EYE
SOMETHING STARTING WITH THE LETTER

It's a
Ghost

I SPY WITH MY LITTLE EYE
SOMETHING STARTING WITH THE LETTER

It's a
Haunted House

I SPY WITH MY LITTLE EYE
SOMETHING STARTING WITH THE LETTER

It's an Insect

I SPY WITH MY LITTLE EYE
SOMETHING STARTING WITH THE LETTER

It's a
Jingle bells

I SPY WITH MY LITTLE EYE
SOMETHING STARTING WITH THE LETTER

It's a
Key

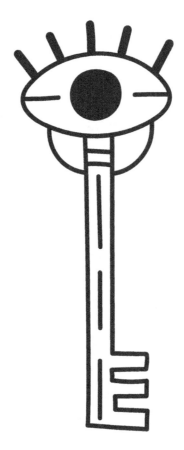

I SPY WITH MY LITTLE EYE
SOMETHING STARTING WITH THE LETTER

It's a
Lollipop

Thank You for Reading!

I want to personally thank you for choosing this book and supporting my work. Your purchase means the world to me, and I truly hope this book brought joy and creativity to your Halloween season!

To show my appreciation, I'd like to offer you something special:

Unlock Exclusive Discounts & Special Offers!

As a thank you for being an awesome reader, I'm offering exclusive discounts on my best-selling books! Just sign up for my email list to unlock:

- 20% off your next book purchase
- Early access to new releases
- Special offers and promotions just for subscribers

To claim your discount and discover more exciting reads, simply scan the QR code below or visit:

kerriwenna.com

You'll also receive Free Bonus content and be the first to hear about exciting new books for your family to enjoy!

I SPY WITH MY LITTLE EYE
SOMETHING STARTING WITH THE LETTER

It's a Monster

I SPY WITH MY LITTLE EYE
SOMETHING STARTING WITH THE LETTER

It's a Nest

I SPY WITH MY LITTLE EYE
SOMETHING STARTING WITH THE LETTER

It's an Owl

I SPY WITH MY LITTLE EYE
SOMETHING STARTING WITH THE LETTER

It's a Potion

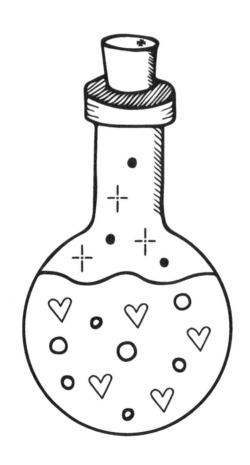

I SPY WITH MY LITTLE EYE SOMETHING STARTING WITH THE LETTER

It's a Quilt

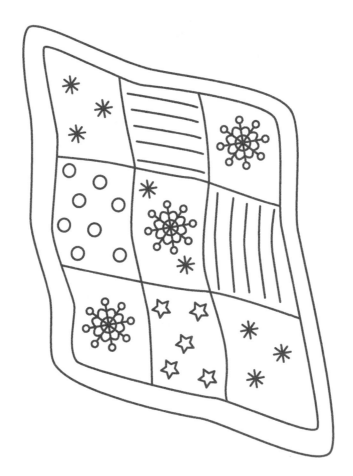

I SPY WITH MY LITTLE EYE
SOMETHING STARTING WITH THE LETTER

It's a Reaper

I SPY WITH MY LITTLE EYE
SOMETHING STARTING WITH THE LETTER

It's a Scarecrow

I SPY WITH MY LITTLE EYE
SOMETHING STARTING WITH THE LETTER

It's a Torch

I SPY WITH MY LITTLE EYE
SOMETHING STARTING WITH THE LETTER

It's an Umbrella

I SPY WITH MY LITTLE EYE
SOMETHING STARTING WITH THE LETTER

It's a Vampire

I SPY WITH MY LITTLE EYE
SOMETHING STARTING WITH THE LETTER

It's a Witch

I SPY WITH MY LITTLE EYE
SOMETHING STARTING WITH THE LETTER

It's a
Xylophone

I SPY WITH MY LITTLE EYE SOMETHING STARTING WITH THE LETTER

It's a Yogurt

I SPY WITH MY LITTLE EYE
SOMETHING STARTING WITH THE LETTER

It's a Zombie

I HOPE YOU ENJOYED!

Congratulations, Little Explorer!

You've completed your Halloween adventure with flying colors!

You've sharpened your observation skills, ignited your creativity, and uncovered hidden treasures on every page. We hope you had a bewitching time with 'I Spy Halloween.'

LEAVE US A FEEDBACK

Don't forget to share your thoughts with us!

We'd love to hear about your child's adventure. Your feedback means the world to us and helps other parents discover the magic of this book.

Share your thoughts and inspire others to embark on their Halloween journey too!

Made in the USA
Las Vegas, NV
20 September 2024